A Humble Life

Plain Poems

A Humble Life

Plain Poems

Written by **Linda Oatman High**

Illustrated by **Bill Farnsworth**

Eerdmans Books for Young Readers

Grand Rapids, Michigan / Cambridge, U.K.

Text © 2001 by Linda Oatman High
Illustrations © 2001 by Bill Farnsworth

Published 2001 by Eerdmans Books for Young Readers
An imprint of Wm. B. Eerdmans Publishing Company
255 Jefferson S.E., Grand Rapids, Michigan 49503
P.O. Box 163, Cambridge CB3 9PU U.K.

Printed in Hong Kong

01 02 03 04 05 06 07 08   8 7 6 5 4 3 2 1

Library of Congress Cataloging-in-Publication Data
High, Linda Oatman
A humble life: plain poems/written by Linda Oatman High; illustrated by Bill Farnsworth.
p. cm.
ISBN 0-8028-5207-6 (alk. paper)
1. Pennsylvania Dutch Country (Pa.)—Juvenile poetry.
2. Pennsylvania Dutch—Juvenile poetry.
3. Children's poetry, American.
[1. Pennsylvania Dutch—Poetry. 2. American poetry.]
I. Farnsworth, Bill. II. Title.
PS3558.I3628 H86 2001
811'.54—dc21
2001023036

The illustrations were painted in oil on linen.
The text type was set in Weiss.

A Humble Life

A humble life
is mine,
and it's a fine existence,
rich with simple gifts
and plain innocence,
pure as clean rain trickling
upon our freshly-painted picket
fence.

Spring, summer, fall,
and winter,
I sing the good hymns,
trusting in God, safe,
in faith, with the One
who created me.

Come Spring

Come spring,
honey butter sun
spreads,
its bread
the emerald buds
of new bloom.

Sprays of bouquets
flinging a maze
of ruffles and lace,
blazing,
a baby's breath
like candy tuft
in the sun,
come spring.

Brand-New Lamb

A sheep bleats
seeking me,
as she
bears breech
a brand-new lamb.

Arriving feet-first,
the crying sweet lamb is birthed,
with my striving hands
guiding her fleece
into this bright world.

Curly pearl-colored wool
full of mats and tangled,
the mother wrangles angrily,
nudging the lamb to stand,
and then quickly licks my hand,
smudged eyes shining
grudging thanks
for my guidance —
a shepherd
bringing a new ewe
into spring mountain dew.

Fishing In The Creek

Fishing in the creek,
seeking bites on my line,
I sigh,
hungry for a pan-fried trout.

Baited with mayfly and jig,
big earthworms squirming
in the bucket,
I cast behind a pine,
near my one-room school,
and the line squiggles
with a nibble.

I wait,
patient,
and then troll again.

When the pole bends,
I yank from my seat on the bank,
catching the fattest fish
in the creek,
stocked
just last week.

In the springtime sunlight,
the sleek trout shines —
shades of the rainbow,
eyes like jeweled fire.

I pray
the fish doesn't swim
away,
on this great April day.

Sowing Seeds

Sowing seeds
in pleasing rows,
we know
the reason
for planting season
is to grow.

Crowing roosters,
boosting sleepy spirits,
keep us working,
tilling fertile earth,
filling moist dirt
with germs of kernels,
starting seeds
to feed
our family.

Come Summer

Come summer,
early sunshine swirls
a blue-milk sky
over newly-turned earth,
as I help
birth a calf
in the morning.

Light brown
and velvety-white
downy coat soaked
as she awoke,
hurled, into this world,
the baby cow bows down
beneath her mother's
rough pink tongue.

Mouth like silk,
the calf suckles milk
like that she'll one day give,
swallowing,
wallowing in love,
come summer.

On Sabbath Summer Mornings

For worship service
on Sabbath summer mornings,
glorious horses clip-clop to church,
pulling clattering black buggies
filled with big families of
chattering, slicked children.

Dressed in Sunday best,
we sing joyful praises
to our Creator,
sometimes eating preaching pies
of sweet dried apples
to keep us quiet and hushed,
not whispering,
during the long sermons
of the bishop.

Outside,
tied in sun-dappled lines
to hitching posts,
tails twitching flies,
the horses adore the Lord,
for he has provided
all needs and treats —
water and oats,
apples and carrots,
brown sugar on Sabbath
summer mornings.

Muggy Summer Nights

Muggy summer nights,
when winged lightning
bugs blink
and chipper crickets
twirl and chirp,
thickening the hot soggy sky
with firefly light
and cricket song,
we sleep snug and deep,
sweating, yet protected,
content, using no electric
for air, illumination, or music.

Patient, soothed by
the smooth shine of ancient moon
and starry sparkled promise afar,
we wait,
entertained by nature in slumber,
until we awaken,
cooled by thunder,
rumbling,
and rain.

Corn

Corn —
Silver Queen,
sweet yellow and white
grows boldly in rows
upon green rows
of tall splendid stalks
stretching to Heaven.

Each evening,
when the sleepy sky
turns purple with streaks,
I pluck ripe ears from stalks,
tossing corn into a tin bucket,
then husking, shucking
tassels, silk, and green leaves
from sun-sweetened kernels.

We cook the cleaned corn
in a hot boiling pot,
slather with fresh churned butter,
salt and pepper gently,
and then,
with grace upon us,
we eat,
lips salty and sweet,
grateful in our hearts
for corn.

Come Fall

Come fall,
tall stalks are chopped down,
brown and dried on crackled ground.
Silos are filled,
fields gilded golden,
ponds rippled yet still.

Getting ready for winter,
we pickle and cure,
can and preserve,
the last of fresh vegetables
and juicy fruits,
lining cellar shelves
with good food.

Tall trees drop leaves
and our spotted dog frolics,
rollicking in high piles
of autumn's baubles,
every leaf a free flower,
come fall.

Barn Raising Day

Baking pies
for barn raising day,
we pray
that no lightning strikes
again.

Hens cluck,
men flock outside,
side by side,
rising high into slate-gray sky,
working hard,
building a barn.

Hammers pound nails,
pails of morning milk are drunk,
lard-fried doughnuts dunked,
as the men join together,
building a barn
to withstand winter weather.

Feathers flapping,
hens are cackling,
spackling the air
with the carefree chatter of chickens,
as children and women
crowd in the kitchen,
shooing blue-winged flies,
singing hymns as they bring
new warm shoofly pies
and hot chicken potpie
to the men outside.

Thanksgiving Dinner

Thanksgiving dinner,
blessed by our Lord,
we add extra boards
to our long wooden table.

Able to say grace first,
I burst with gratitude
beholden to God
for his golden goods.

Roasted turkey and stuffing,
fluffy whipped potatoes with gravy,
wavy red sauce
of cranberries,
glossy green peas,
we eat, hungry,
as our other turkeys gobble,
wobbly-legged
and grateful, too,
outside.

Pumpkins and Mums

At harvest time,
Saturday gathering,
a gentle west wind is scattering
mens' black hats
like slow flapping bats.

Pumpkins and mums —
purple and orange, burnt rust and yellow —
mellow in marigold-carrot sun,
are sold for fun and money
collected in cans
at our sunny roadside stand.

Regular customers come,
fussily choosing best colors of mums
and the roundest pumpkins for carving,
as fast cars hum
past, and the day seems to last,
forever.

Come Winter

Come winter,
black cinders of coal
darken the old
stove's oval window,
as fire glows
yellow-orange within.

I quilt, stitching patterns
upon fabric
fat with batting
as our white-furred cat naps
purring, lazy and cozy
by the stove.

Snow floats outside,
making soft lacy shapes
on the frosty windowpane,
piling high
as the cat and I
hide inside,
come winter.

Shivery Winter Mornings

I shiver on winter mornings,
quivering, as slivers of ice
slice the frigid gray sky,
cutting my skin as I begin
morning chores.

Collecting eggs,
milking the cows,
frowning as I slop the hogs,
I slog through slush,
rushing to mix mush
for hungry clucking chickens.

I shiver as sleet splinters
the silent winter sky,
wishing that I
were inside,
by the fire.

Tired of cold,
I fold my arms,
running across the farmyard
to the warm kitchen,
where breakfast is ready —
yesterday's best eggs,
fresh-skimmed milk,
crisp sizzling bacon making
my stomach grumble
as a snowman
smiles
outside.

When the Pond Freezes Solid

When the pond freezes solid,
we skate,
skimming thick ice with thin silver blades,
making heart shapes and figure-eights,
playing wild hockey with puck and wooden sticks,
creating a ruckus on the ice.

Sharpening old blades dulled by falls,
we take breaks by the bonfire,
drinking lots of hot chocolate brought by friends.

Lacing our skates,
we return to blade-sliced ice,
enticing Bessie the crazy cow
to learn to walk, dazed, clumsily,
upon the frozen water.

White Winter Nights

Chicken corn soup
scooped steaming
from the huge kettle
whets my appetite
mightily on white winter nights.

Kerosene lanterns
burn, the sheen gleaming
upon the plain ceiling
as we eat,
greeting relatives visiting
overnight.

Warm whoopie pies
of moist-cake chocolate
and sweet white cream
are dessert,
and finally it's time
for playing board games
by the lantern's light
on white winter nights.

Author's note

All my life, I've lived in Pennsylvania Dutch Country. Here in Lancaster County, there are many groups of Plain People, a term that includes all the unique branches of the Mennonite and Amish communities. While each group has its own set of rules, the main philosophy of the Plain People is a desire to set themselves apart from the world. Therefore, they seek to live humble lives and rely on their faith in God to carry them day by day and season by season.

— LINDA OATMAN HIGH